# Mimi and Violet Not Getting Along

Written by
Lisa Menzel

Illustrated by
Taranggana

This book is dedicated to my beautiful family.

Thank you for your unconditional love and support.

I am eternally grateful that you are in my life.

You are my gift.

One rainy afternoon, Mimi and Violet were playing together with their blocks on the floor, while Mum and Dad were having a cup of tea in the kitchen.
"What are you building girls?" asked Dad.
"A house for my doll" answered Mimi excitedly.
"I'm building a castle for my princess" replied Violet proudly.

Mimi picked up a yellow block to add to her house.

"Hey, I need that block, don't snatch!" shouted Violet with an angry look on her face.

"I didn't snatch... I had it first" Mimi yelled back.

Mimi didn't like the way Violet yelled at her. Now Mimi felt angry. Mum and Dad could hear that Mimi and Violet were not getting along but they waited to see if the girls could work it out for themselves.

Violet quickly took a block that was near Mimi.

"That's mine!" shouted Mimi. Mimi's angry face quickly turned into a sad face then back to an angry face. Mimi felt hot all over her body and her heart was beating fast. She snatched back the block from Violet's hand.

Now Violet's angry face turned into a sad face and she burst out crying. All of a sudden, Violet's whole body felt hot and tingly and her head was going to pop! Violet felt sad and angry that Mimi snatched the block from her hand. Just then, Violet pushed Mimi and she fell to the floor. Mimi felt shocked that Violet had pushed her. That really hurt her feelings so she started to cry!

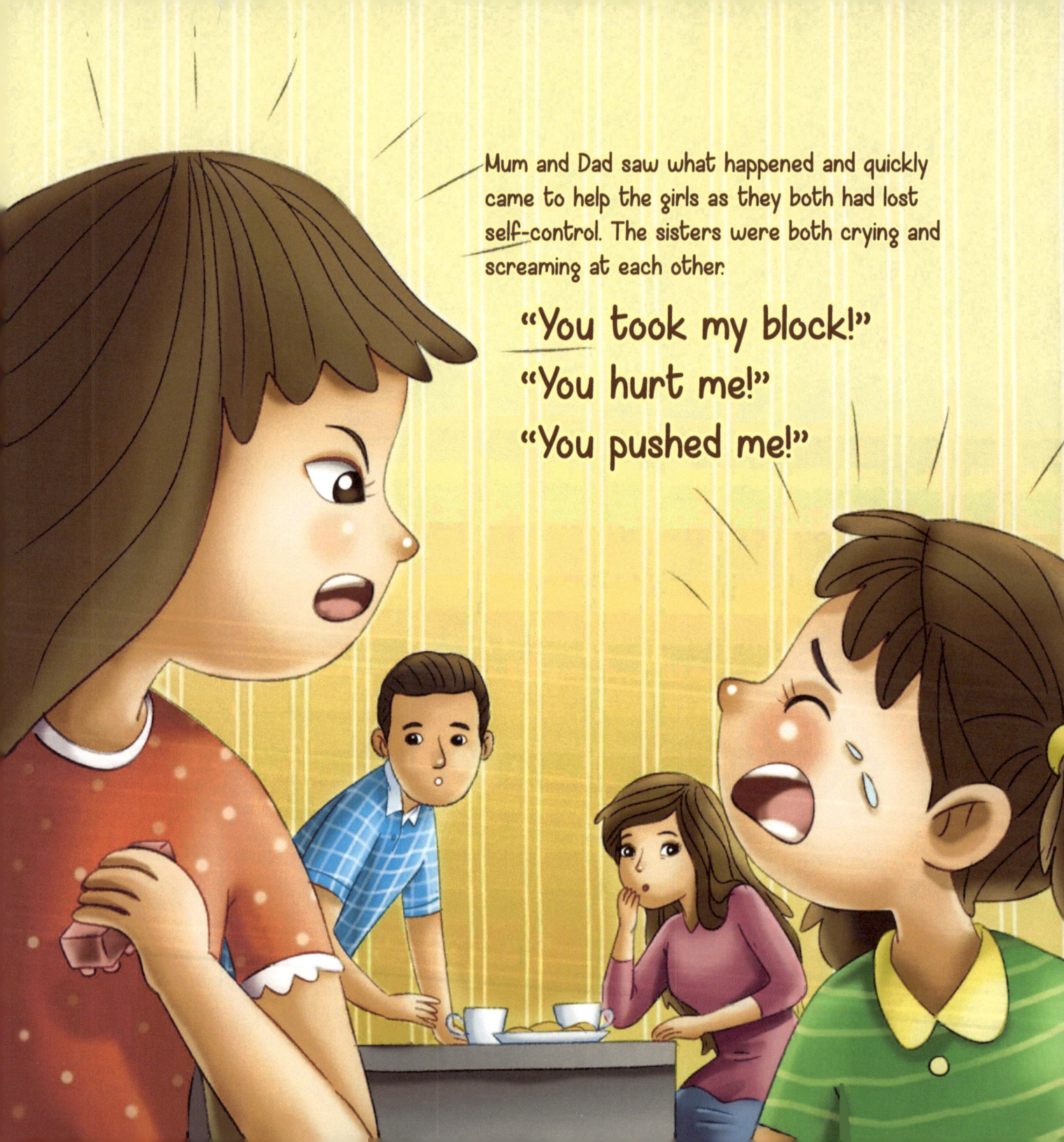

Mum and Dad saw what happened and quickly came to help the girls as they both had lost self-control. The sisters were both crying and screaming at each other.

"You took my block!"

"You hurt me!"

"You pushed me!"

Mum and Dad sat down on the floor with the girls and asked them both to take 3 big deep breaths to help them calm down.
Dad asked both girls to look at him and he said with a calm but firm voice:
"We don't push or put our hands on anyone, especially when we are angry. That behaviour is inappropriate".

"What happened Violet that made you feel so angry?" queried Mum.
Violet didn't answer. She had tears in her eyes and felt scared that she was going to be in big trouble.
Mum then tried a different approach.
"Tell me Violet, where in your body did you feel angry?"
Violet had a puzzled look on her face and thought about the question for a while.

Then she answered "I felt really hot and tingly all over my body and in my head.
I was sad and angry that Mimi snatched the block from my hands."

"It's OK to feel angry"
Mum told Violet.
"Anger is a normal feeling.
You just need to express your anger appropriately.
Pushing Mimi was very inappropriate.
What could you have done differently
instead of using your hands?"
asked Mum.

Violet replied:
"I could use my words and tell her to give it back or ask Mum or Dad for help."

"Great suggestions Violet" encouraged Mum.

She leaned over and gave Violet a big hug.

Then Mum gave Violet a new strategy to help her manage her angry feelings.

"You could also look for clues in your body that will tell you that you are feeling angry, just like you said you felt hot and tingly. Then you can stop, take a deep breath and think about making an appropriate choice about your behaviour" said Mum.

"Now look at Mimi's face and tell us what she might be feeling?

Does Mimi look happy or sad?" quizzed Mum.

Mimi was still sobbing.

Violet looked down at the floor instead of looking at Mimi.

She felt ashamed of pushing and hurting her sister.

Violet then looked at her sister and mumbled "she looks sad".

"How would you feel if Mimi pushed you?" Mum asked.

"Sad" Violet replied.

"That's another clue to make better choices Violet.

Feeling what it would be like if you were the one who was hurt,

as if you were in her shoes" explained Mum.

Dad gave Mimi a big squeeze and helped her to stop crying.
"Take a big deep breath in and out and try to calm down" suggested Dad.
"Come on, I will do it with you...big breath in...and big breath out. Let's do that again".
Mimi noticed that her heart beat slowed down.
She stopped crying.
Mimi was now calm.

"Yes, that's a great idea. How about you look at Mimi and do that now?" encouraged Dad.
Violet looked at Mimi and said: "I'm sorry for pushing you Mimi.
I didn't mean to hurt you" Violet leaned over and gave her sister
a big hug.

Mimi felt better. Mimi replied "That's OK Violet. I'm sorry too. Let's play with the blocks again". The two sisters were happy again. They shared the blocks and built one big castle for their toys. Dad looked at Mimi and Violet and said: "It's great to see you girls getting along".

# Helpful information for Parents

This book is part of a series that helps families explore childhood social-emotional development. It is important for children to learn positive and appropriate problem-solving & coping skills so they can grow and develop into highly functioning adults. These are life-long skills so it is important to teach children early.

You can help your child by:

- Reading this book with your child to open conversations about **thoughts, feelings and behaviours**.
Anger is a NORMAL emotion like feeling happy or sad, however it is how we express anger through our behaviour that is either appropriate or inappropriate. Be non-judgmental and clearly distinguish behaviour with language such as: "appropriate" and "inappropriate".

- **Lead by example**. Children learn their social skills by observing other's interactions. Be aware of your own problem-solving and conflict resolution methods. Teach children ways to 'problem-solve' and resolve conflict by encouraging them to use their words and provide them with the language base to help them articulate their emotions.

- Encourage **self-awareness** as this will provide 'clues' as to how children can problem-solve. Behaviour is driven by emotions, and emotions are driven by thoughts. Therefore, it is important to understand 'self-talk' and the physiological symptoms it causes such as an increased heart rate and sweaty palms. This is an opportunity to STOP, BREATHE and CALM DOWN to THINK CLEARLY about an appropriate response.

- Encourage children to express their emotions through art and craft as well as playing outside with sporting equipment. This is a **safe and appropriate** option of dealing with angry feelings and a great opportunity to play and connect with children.

- Seek **professional counselling** if you need further strategies, support or assistance. There are effective evidence-based therapeutic approaches that can help your family.

Anger is a secondary emotion. Underneath **anger is a primary emotion** such as hurt, disappointment, sadness, jealousy and frustration. Be curious and try to understand what is behind your child's anger. This process will help you recognise their primary need and allow you to help your child understand this about themselves and consequently help them to self-regulate their emotions and behaviours.

Teach and guide your child to be **assertive** – a skill that will help them flourish in becoming confident and competent human beings with a strong sense of wellbeing.

Check in with your own emotions the next time you feel angry. Is it GUILT, SHAME, HURT or EMBARASSMENT that is underneath your anger? Reflect on your own feelings and emotions and use this as a learning opportunity for the whole family.

For more information or to contact the Author visit:

**wellwithincounselling.com.au**

www.ingramcontent.com/pod-product-compliance
Lightning Source LLC
Chambersburg PA
CBHW042052030526
44107CB00090B/1554